INVESTIGATING MYSTERIOUS PLACES

EASTER ISLAND
STONE GIANTS OF THE PACIFIC

by Allan Morey

CAPSTONE PRESS
a capstone imprint

Published by Capstone Press, an imprint of Capstone
1710 Roe Crest Drive, North Mankato, Minnesota 56003
capstonepub.com

Copyright © 2025 by Capstone. All rights reserved. No part of this publication may be reproduced in whole or in part, or stored in a retrieval system, or transmitted in any form or by any means, electronic, mechanical, photocopying, recording, or otherwise, without written permission of the publisher.

Library of Congress Cataloging-in-Publication Data is available on the Library of Congress website.

ISBN: 9781669093411 (hardcover)
ISBN: 9781669093367 (paperback)
ISBN: 9781669093374 (ebook PDF)

Summary: Travel to Easter Island and meet the moai, the huge stone statues that watch over the island! How were these giant figures made and moved by the people of the island long ago? This book takes you on a trip to uncover the secrets of these stone giants. Find out about the island's past, why the moai were built, and how they've lasted so long.

Editorial Credits
Editor: Donald Lemke; Designer: Tracy Davies; Media Researcher: Svetlana Zhurkin; Production Specialist: Katy LaVigne

Image Credits
Alamy: Alto Vintage Images, 13, Gail Mooney-Kelly, 14; Dreamstime: Kadumago Artes, 26; Getty Images: AlbertoLoyo, 21, DeAgostini Picture Library, 25, 27, mikroman6, 17, Mlenny, 5, O. Alamany & E. Vicens, 29, Pavel Tochinsky, 23, Posnov, 7, 18; Newscom: Heritage Images/The Print Collector, 15; Shutterstock: Ada_Maz, 9, Adwo, 24, Aliaksei Hintau (smoke background), 2 and throughout, Anton_Ivanov, 6, Bryan Busovicki, 19, Christian Wilkinson, 8, Galina Barskaya, cover, back cover, 1, Katsiaryna Pleshakova (moai icon), cover and throughout, Peter Hermes Furian, 11, Rainer Lesniewski, 12

Any additional websites and resources referenced in this book are not maintained, authorized, or sponsored by Capstone. All product and company names are trademarks™ or registered® trademarks of their respective holders.

TABLE OF CONTENTS

Chapter One
THE MOAI..4

Chapter Two
ISLAND HISTORY..10

Chapter Three
ANCIENT BELIEFS..16

Chapter Four
MYSTERIES REMAIN..22

GLOSSARY..30
READ MORE..31
INTERNET SITES..31
INDEX..32
ABOUT THE AUTHOR..32

Chapter One

THE MOAI

What are the moai? They are huge stone statues. Moai look like short, squat people with big heads and long noses.

Most of the statues stand about twice as tall as an adult. They may weigh as much as a school bus—or more!

Broken Paro moai lies face down on the ground.

The tallest moai is called Paro. Before it fell, the statue stood more than 32 feet (10 meters) tall. It weighed 90 tons (82 metric tons).

Some of the moai wear hats called pukao.

These were made from red stone.

Where are these strange statues found? Easter Island. The moai were **carved** long ago by ancient **Polynesian** people living on the island.

An Indigenous group performs on Easter Island.

FACT
People living on Easter Island call the island Rapa Nui.

Easter Island is the most remote inhabited island in the world.

Chapter Two

ISLAND HISTORY

Easter Island is in the middle of the South Pacific Ocean. It lies about 2,200 miles (3,500 kilometers) off the coast of Chile, South America.

The island is tiny. It stretches just 14 miles (23 km) long and is only seven miles (11 km) wide. But Easter Island was once home to thousands of people.

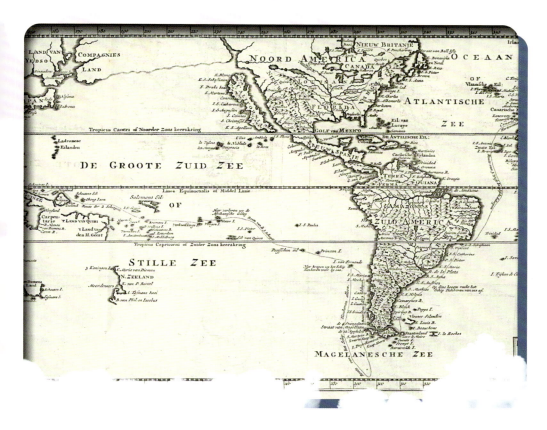

Map showing Jacob Roggeveen's voyage

Dutch explorer Jacob Roggeveen was the first European to step foot on the island. He landed there on Easter Sunday in 1722. That is why it is called Easter Island.

A small group of Polynesian people were the first people to live on the island. Ancient Polynesians traveled the giant South Pacific Ocean in wooden canoes.

A Rapa Nui man with traditional body paint on Easter Island

Ancient Polynesians rowing canoes

They rowed thousands of miles searching for new islands to explore. They found Easter Island about 1,500 years ago.

FACT
At 1,969 feet (600 m), Mount Terevaka is the tallest peak on Easter Island.

Chapter Three

ANCIENT BELIEFS

People have many questions about the **mysterious** moai. They were built long before Jacob Roggeveen arrived on Easter Island. But why?

Archaeologists believe the moai are past chiefs or other important figures. People of the island may have built them believing the statues held the **spirits** of these **ancestors**.

Researchers believe the moai honored Rapa Nui's ancestors.

Around 1,000 moai have been found on the island. Many are not finished. Others never reached their final resting place. Some have even been buried over time.

An unfinished moai on the side of a mountain

Ahu Tongariki has the largest group of moai on Easter Island.

Nearly 300 moai line the island's coast. They are often grouped together on platforms called ahu. Most of these moai stand with their backs to the sea.

Why? So the moai could watch over the people of the island. Ancient peoples living there once believed the moai **protected** them.

FACT

The moai do not have eyes.

The statues have been watching over the Rapa Nui people for hundreds of years.

Chapter Four

MYSTERIES REMAIN

There are still many unsolved mysteries about the moai. How did the people living on the island move them?

These statues were carved from soft **volcanic** rock. But they still weigh many tons. And ancient peoples did not have cranes or semitrailers to move them around.

Tourists looking up at the giant statues

One idea is that the statues were "walked." Ropes were tied to the heads of the moai.

One group in the back kept the moai in the upright position.

Once in place, the moai may have been raised using ropes and wooden poles.

They were then rocked side to side, slowly moving forward. It would have taken a large group of people to move them this way.

Ancient Polynesians moving the moai on Easter Island

Another idea is they were placed on round logs. The moai were then rolled across the island on the logs.

Why did the people of Easter Island stop carving the moai? Archaeologists believe a war broke out. They have found ancient weapons buried on the island.

A Rapa Nui man with a spear

Some questions about the moai may never truly be answered. The moai were built long before Europeans arrived on the island.

Much of what we know about them is based on legends and stories. That is why Easter Island remains such a mysterious place.

Much of Easter Island is now part of the Rapa Nui National Park.

Glossary

ancestor (AN-ses-tor)—a family member who lived a long time ago

archaeologist (ar-kee-OL-uh-jist)—a scientist who studies old things left by people from the past to learn how they lived

carved (KARVD)—cut into something (like wood or stone) to make shapes or designs

mysterious (mis-TEER-ee-us)—something that is very hard to understand or explain

Polynesian (pol-ee-NEE-zhuhn)—related to the islands in the central and southern Pacific Ocean, including the cultures and peoples living there

protected (pruh-TEK-tid)—kept safe from harm or danger

spirit (SPIR-it)—the non-physical part of people, often thought to live on after the body dies

volcanic (vol-KAN-ik)—having to do with volcanoes, which are mountains that can erupt with hot liquid rock

Read More

Bradshaw, Eleanor. *20 things you didn't know about Easter Island.* Buffalo, NY: PowerKids Press, 2024.

Newbauer, Heidi. *Statues of Easter Island.* Mankato, MN: Creative Education, 2025.

Waxman, Laura Hamilton. *Mysteries of Easter Island.* Minneapolis: Lerner Publications, 2018.

Internet Sites

History Channel: Easter Island
history.com/topics/south-america/easter-island

National Geographic: Discover the Mysteries of Easter Island
nationalgeographic.com/travel/world-heritage/article/easter-island

Smithsonian Magazine: The Secrets of Easter Island
smithsonianmag.com/history/the-secrets-of-easter-island-59989046/

Index

ahu, 19
ancestors, 16, 17
archaeologists, 16, 27

Chile, 10

Easter Island, 8, 9, 10–13, 14, 15, 16, 19, 26, 27, 28
size of, 12
location of, 10, 11
map of, 11
Europeans, 13

moai, 4, 6, 7, 8, 16, 17, 18, 19, 20, 21, 22, 23, 24–25, 26, 27, 28

number of, 18, 19
size of, 4, 6
transportation of, 24–26
weight of, 4, 6

Paro, 6
Polynesia
people of, 8, 13–14
pukao, 7

Roggeveen, Jacob, 13, 16

South America, 10
South Pacific Ocean, 10, 11, 14
spirits, 16
stone, 4, 7, 22

About the Author

Some of Allan Morey's favorite childhood memories are from the time he spent on a farm in Wisconsin. Every day he saw cows, chickens, and sheep. He even had a pet pig named Pete. He developed a great appreciation of animals, big and small. Allan currently lives in St. Paul with his family and dogs, Stitch and Enzo, who keep him company while he writes.